My Mommy Had a Miscarriage
copyright © 2017 by Liz Ryan
All rights reserved.
No part of this publication may be reproduced, stored in retrieval system, or transmitted in any form or by any means— electronic, mechanical, digital, photo copy, recording, or any other— except for brief quotations in printed reviews, without the written permission of the publisher. For information regarding permission, contact Liz Ryan at LizRyanAuthor@gmail.com

ISBN-13: 978-0-999257-0-3
ISBN-10: 0-999257-0-4

MY MOMMY HAD A MISCARRIAGE

Written and Illustrated by Liz Ryan

To Our Sweet Little One.
I carry you in my heart.
12-29-2009

In Honor of the babies we didn't get to keep.
They are loved.

My mommy's belly looks like spring.
Just like a flower, our baby grows.
It is the most AMAZING thing!

She says that the baby is our
Little Love Bug,
and I am her C-r-a-a-z-y Daisy.

My mommy sings sweet songs, just like the birdies in my tree.
So happy, wild, and free.

Our Little Love Bug dances in her belly while I stand on Mommy's feet.

We dance through the house and Daddy does big leaps.

It is so exciting to hear the baby's heart beat.
It sounds just like a drum... "baBOOM, baBOOM!"

Our Little Love Bug makes music for Mommy, Daddy, and Me.

Summertime is here, and that means it's time for an airport picnic.
We watch the planes come in and the clouds float by.
My mommy says she knows one thing...

She loves us both as high as the sky.

I think our baby will be smiley, silly, and like my toys.
My mommy thinks our baby might be a ninja,
with all of those flutter kicks, flippity flips.

I wonder if our baby
will be a girl or a boy.

I guess we will just have to wait
until we meet our Little Love Bug
on that special trip.

The very next day,
my mommy looked different.
Daddy just stayed with her
and gave her a hug.

I knew she was sad,
it was quite apparent.

Her eyes had tears.
One by one,
they started to fall off her cheeks.
I was afraid to go anywhere,
so I stayed near.
Her tears continued to pour
for weeks and weeks.

My mommy's tears drizzled and dripped, reminding me of the rain.

She cried, cried, and couldn't explain.

Then, she cried some more.
I bet it was enough to make a puddle on the floor.

My daddy cried too.
He said sometimes, that's the only thing you can do.

My mommy and I sat down quietly, with my daddy right by my side.
She wrapped me in a hug and said I'm her Crazy Daisy.

Then she squeezed me even tighter and looked me in the eyes,
she said our Little Love Bug in her belly had just died.

So we loved and we cried.

I screamed and I tried,

I did not understand.

This was not the plan.

That baby was ours,

no matter how small!

You can't tell me otherwise,

you just can't at all!

What did this mean?
Why did our baby leave her belly,
and not stay?
We sang and we talked.
We danced and we walked.
All with our Little Love Bug,
who I just want to give a big hug.

I have all of these questions stuck in my head.

Some days I leave them be, so my mommy can rest in bed.

But other days they come roaring out.

I just can't keep them in, I have to ask now!

Where is our baby, Mommy? Where is our Little Love Bug?

Other days I start to feel funny inside, with knots in my belly, tangled up like I'm on a wild ride.

But then my mommy comes over and hugs me so tight.
She says she feels tangled up too, even at night.
So we cry together. Really hard.
I wish we could have a redo and a restart.

It feels good to cry.

Just like jumping in puddles on a hot summer day.

We let it all out and stare up at the sky.

My mommy says she is looking for a rainbow

to know that things will be okay.

Some days,

my mommy's shadow

carries her heart.

Then some days, we run into people
who don't know what to say.

Their words come out all twisty and turvey,
coming out all the wrong way.

Their words hurt my mommy and me.

Just like a hero, my daddy swoops in,
covering us with his cape of protection.

Some days, I can see my mommy start to change a bit.
Like the leaves of a tree turning from green, to red, then orange and yellow.

The wind starts to blow the leaves and they hit,
right down to the ground they swirl and flow.

Little things remind us of our baby every day.

Like the clouds in the sky and the songs that we sing.

Boy do I wish our baby had stayed!

Some days, we go to the beach for a break from the cold.

We play in the sand and dig in our feet

as we watch the big waves roll off the beautiful sea.

The waves crash down, one on top of another,
calming down before they get to me.
They remind me of the hurts in my heart that seem to hover.
I wish these hurts would just break free!

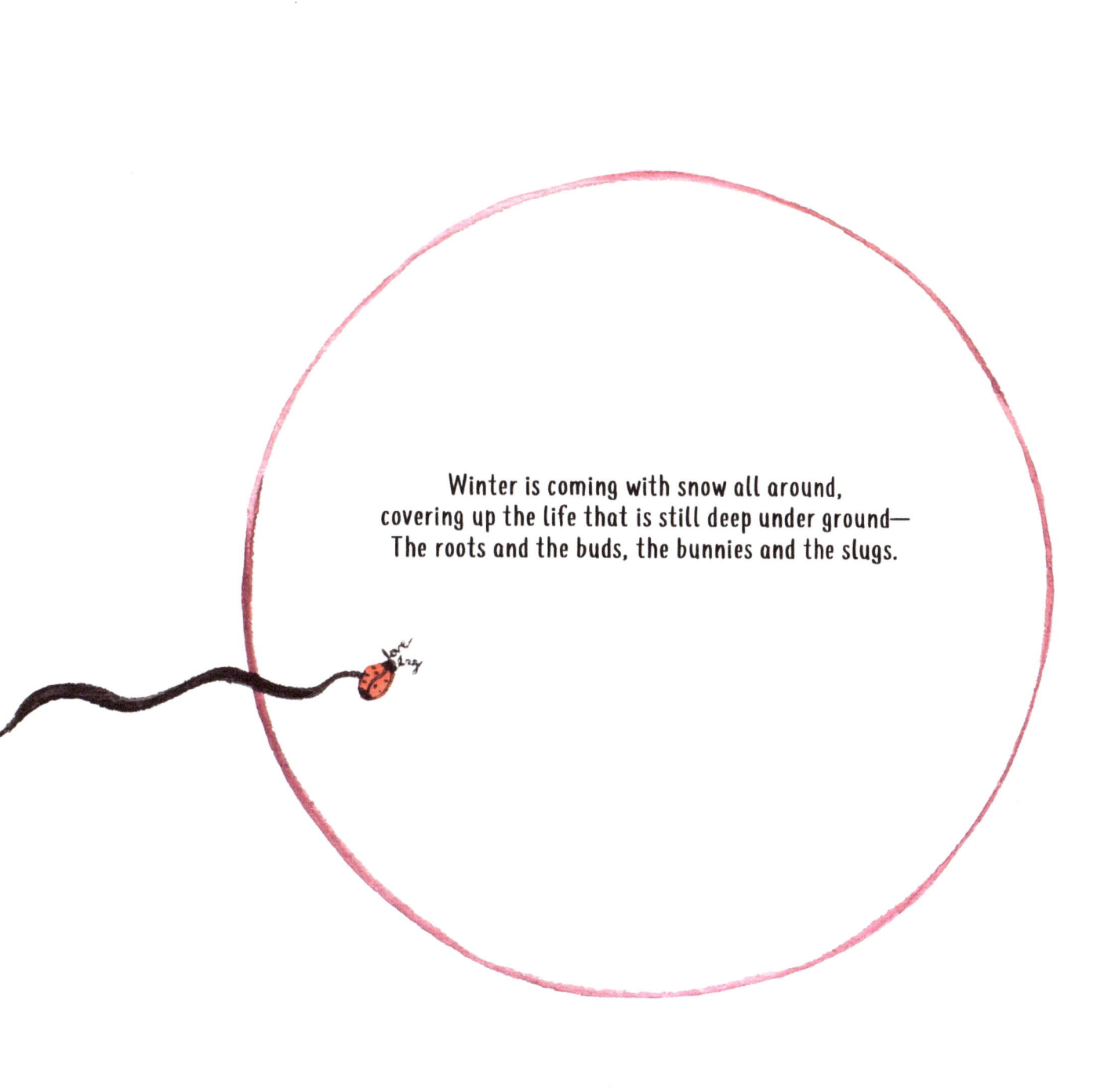

Winter is coming with snow all around,
covering up the life that is still deep under ground—
The roots and the buds, the bunnies and the slugs.

Spring is near and life is in bloom.
I hear my mommy whisper...

"LIFE NEVER STOPPED, WHEN WE LOST YOU,
AND WE KEPT GROWING AS A FAMILY, WITH ALL WE HAVE BEEN THROUGH."

I knew she was talking to our baby,
even though I was in the other room.

We all have Love Buckets,
and mommy's was empty,
in need of some filling.

So, my daddy and I walked in
and surprised her
with squeezies and huggles,
until her bucket was almost spilling.

We made her smile,
even though things still felt like a blur.

My daddy says nature is a reminder of many little things.

The clouds still move and the birds still sing.

The sun still shines, and the moon still rises.

Some plants grow so very tall.

While others
never make it out of the ground,
and remain little,
or not at all.

Our baby would have fit so perfect in our arms.

But for now will have to fit only in our hearts.

We will keep our baby's light burning ever so brightly,

speaking life to our memories, so we never forget.

Our sweet Little Love Bug, who we never met.

My mommy always says,
"My Little Love Bug and Crazy Daisy, you BOTH will always be!"

We are woven together, by the heart strings of loss.

"The pain of loss will pass eventually. Let yourself feel the pain and let yourself grieve."

• SHELLEY B. • CALEB 9-1-1998 • 5-3-2002

"It's important to grieve— open the door and take it all in… Just don't live there. Remember the door. Come and go. Make hope your home."

• ANNA K. • EMMERY, LUCA, MARA, & VERA

"An empty womb, a lost child— it's like waking up in the middle of the night. Scared like a child, looking for something you've lost… I don't think you ever feel okay with not finding that one thing you lost. But the day does eventually come. That brokeness is a part of you. It will change the way you view life and loss forever."

• ALYSSA H. • 8-9-2012 ELEVEN WEEKS

"This happens to more women than you think. Talk about your feelings to anyone who will listen, and you will find unexpected comfort pouring from the women around you."

• KATIE O.H. • BABY DARBY, THIRFTEEN WEEKS

"It's okay to hurt. Your heart WILL heal. We shall meet again, little one."

• SARAH AND DANIEL H. • LUCAS 7-2-2013 TWENTY-ONE WEEKS

"I trust in the divine order of the universe. I had to trust in our path and surrender control… even when we don't understand our path, or it's painful. Trusting that no matter where my pregnancies and births take me and my babies, we are going to be okay."

• AMY G. • 12-25-2015 FIVE WEEKS

ABOUT THE AUTHOR

Years after suffering a miscarriage, Liz Ryan realized that there was not a book that addressed miscarriage, as a resource for young children. She decided to use the experience written on her heart, and wrote and illustrated "My Mommy Had a Miscarriage," for families, friends, and communities to walk through together. Her hope is to open the lines of communication, in a way that children can understand, as well as adults who have not walked this path.

JOIN OUR COMMUNITY FOR SUPPORT

Facebook: Author Liz Ryan
Instagram: Author.Liz.Ryan

www.ingramcontent.com/pod-product-compliance
Lightning Source LLC
Chambersburg PA
CBHW042124040426
42450CB00002B/62